Staying Alive

Kat Roberts

Staying Alive was first performed at StageSpace, Pleasance, London, on 10 November 2015

Staying Alive

Kat Roberts

CAST

Mary	Rachel Nott
Jack	Alexander Pankhurst
Jenn	Eleanor Burke
Nathan	Brendan Jones
Portia/Sarah/Social Worker	Emily Rae
Will/Administrator	Stephen Ashmore-Blakely
Voice of Tom	Lolly Mortimore

CREATIVE TEAM

Director	Ellie Pitkin
Designer	Michelle Bristow
Sound & Lighting Designer	Andrew Crane
Assistant Director	Marcus Bazley
Associate Producers	Iasha Chapman
	Charlotte Discombe
	Emma Griffiths
	Helen Johnson
	Nicole Locke
	Richard Stratton
	Nick Tatchell
	Vikki Weston

Marketing Design by **Matt Roberts at euphita**
(**www.euphita.com**)

Special thanks to **Euphita** and **AKT Productions**

Staying Alive premiered at StageSpace Pleasance London, 10-29th November 2015, licensed by arrangement with The Agency (London) Ltd, 24 Pottery Lane, London W11 4LZ, *email*: info@theagency.co.uk.

BIOGRAPHIES

RACHEL NOTT | MARY
Training: The Poor School.

Credits include: *Billy Liar* (Coopers Arms); *Pirates!* (Polka); *Saturday, Sunday, Monday* (Workhouse Theatre); *The Memory of Water* (Rose and Crown); *FourPlay* (Hen & Chickens); *The Bill* (Talkback Television). Rachel is also a co-producer for Four Eyes and the Peach.

ALEXANDER PANKHURST | JACK
Training: Royal Holloway University of London.

Recent cedits include: Demetrius and Bottom in *A Midsummer Night's Dream*; Boy in *Panther*; Gerry in *Dearly Departed*; Mal in *Captcha*; Arnold in *I'll take a Dozen Accountants... with Sprinkles*; Christopher Marlowe in *Death of Marlowe*; Major Steve in *Love in Freefall*; Ash in *A Million Things*; Borachio in *Much Ado About Nothing*; Mercutio in *Romeo and Juliet*; Valentine in *Two Gentlemen of Verona*; Thomas Carnacki in *Audience with the Ghostfinder*; Tom in *Rabbit*; Richard III in *The Shakespeare Conspiracy*; Jamie in *Airport* and Dr Alfred Prunesquallor in *Gormenghast: Titus Groan*.

BRENDAN JONES | NATHAN
Training: The Poor School.

Film and TV credits include: The bell boy in *Bright Young Things* directed by Stephen Fry and John Houseman in *Days That Shook The World* directed by David Bartlett.

Brendan's theatre credits include Eugene in *The Wolf* directed by Jamie Harper, and Joan Miro in *Café Duende* directed by Jamie Harper.

ELEANOR BURKE | JENN
Training: The Poor School.

Theatre credits include: Beverly in *Abigail's Party* (The Art of Dining); *News Revue*, *Sketchageddon Live* (Canal Cafe); Octavius in *Julius Caesar* (Brockley Jack); *Timbre* (Torn Apart Theatre); *The Women at The Tomb, La Ronde* (Theatre Collection) and for Blackshaw Theatre Company: *Alice Springs, Staying Alive* (Blackshaw New Writing Nights).

Film and TV credits include: *Kon Tiki* (RPC & Nordisk Film); *Grey Cafe* (The Bootleg Universe); *Suspect 13, Coming Out* (Shoot Me Films); *Newsnight* (BBC); *First Light* (Fervent Films); *The Wine Picker* (Screaming Eagle Productions); *The Violinist, Four Tongues* (The Ideas Factory); *Thomas The Tank Engine & Friends* (Red Caravan); *Tequila* (Eternal Media Productions); *Bunking Off* (Nic Penrake Films).

STEPHEN ASHMORE-BLAKELY | WILL/ADMINISTRATOR
Training: The Poor School.

Theatre credits include: Dr Dorn in *The Seagull* (Minack); u/s Jack, Colin, Simeon in *Life of Riley* (No. 1 tour); Bob in *Tea & Filth* (Hen & Chickens); Mike in *The Memory of Water* (Rose & Crown); David in *Take It or Leave It* (SNTH); Adrian in *If the Cap Fits* (Etcetera); Peter Quince in *A Midsummer Night's Dream* (Figheldean Outdoor); u/s Andy, Bill, Gerald in *Woman in Mind* (Vaudeville); and 'Prince' in *Romeo & Juliet*, (Pacific Playhouse).

Film & TV credits include: *2nd Class*, and *Revealed: Britain's Nazi King*

EMILY RAE | PORTIA/SARAH/SOCIAL WORKER
Training: The Guildford School of Acting.

Credits during training include Masha in *Three Sisters*, Hermia in *A Midsummer Night's Dream*, Leonardo's Wife in *Blood Wedding and* Midas' Daughter in *Metamorphoses*.

Professionally, Emily has completed two UK tours with Quantum Theatre and Blunderbus Theatre Company. She has also been invited to perform at The Hospital Club in Covent Garden. Emily has performed as Alice in Blackshaw's production of *Alice In Wonderland* at the Wandsworth Arts Festival 2014 and 2015. As well as helping to develop several projects at The London Theatre Workshop, she has recently completed a three-week run of *The Tempest* playing Antonio.

KAT ROBERTS | WRITER
Kat Roberts studied Drama and Creative Writing at Royal Holloway University; English Literature at The Open University and Acting at the Poor School. Kat has also completed both Tamasha's Writing Masterclass with Ella Hickson, and Stephen Jeffrey's Advances in Scriptwriting Course (RADA). Her writing credits include short plays *The Second Stage of Grief* produced by The Goat Theatre Company (2012); *Take me* (2014) and *Age UK* (2015); both for Blackshaw Theatre's New Writing Nights. *Staying Alive* is her first full-length play in production. Kat is currently completing her second full-length piece, *Canary*, and researching the junior doctor contract row.

ELLIE PITKIN | DIRECTOR
Ellie is the Managing & Artistic Director of Blackshaw Theatre, which she founded in May 2010. Directing credits include *Arcadia* by Tom Stoppard (2006) and *Our Country's Good* by Timberlake Wertenbaker (2009). With Blackshaw, Ellie has directed *Gormenghast: Titus Groan* (April 2012, The Actors' Church, Covent Garden); *Audience with the Ghost Finder* (May & Oct 2013, Selkirk Upstairs and Etcetera) by M. J. Starling; *Character* by Florence Vincent (May 2014 & March 2015, Selkirk Upstairs/Tristan Bates); *Alice in Wonderland* (May 2014, May 2015 & July 2015, Selkirk Upstairs/Battersea Library/The British Home); *Staying Alive* by Kat Roberts (January 2015, Pleasance Theatre).

A graduate in Theatre Studies from Royal Holloway University (2008), Ellie also comperes Blackshaw's regular New Writing Nights.

MICHELLE BRISTOW | SET & COSTUME DESIGNER

Michelle has assisted on set and costume for previous Blackshaw productions: *Alice in Wonderland* by Richard Stratton (2014 & 2015), *Character* by Florence Vincent (2014 & 2015); *Audience with the Ghost Finder* by M. J. Starling (2013). She also designed set and costume for Blackshaw's *Halloween Tales* (2014), featuring a candlelit reading and *Fetch* by Duncan Gates.

Since graduating from Wimbledon College of Arts (2014) with a degree in Costume Design, Michelle designed Blackshaw's Showcase of *Staying Alive* in January (2015), and more recently has been working with Fourth Monkey Theatre Company. Michelle is also experienced in the production of dance pieces, and has spent time working in the Costume Department at the London Contemporary Dance School.

ANDREW CRANE | SOUND & LIGHTING DESIGNER

Andrew is a graduate in Drama and Theatre Studies from Royal Holloway University (2012), and has worked as a sound designer and technician for Blackshaw Theatre since 2012. Sound Design credits include *Alice in Wonderland* by Richard Stratton (2014 & 2015), *Character* by Florence Vincent (2014), and *Fetch* by Duncan Gates (2014).

For Blackshaw Theatre's Arts Hour on Wandsworth Radio, Andrew has edited several radio plays including the radio adaptation of *Audience with the Ghost Finder* by M. J. Starling (2015), and is currently working on a serialised adaptation of *Great Expectations* by Marcus Bazley.

MARCUS BAZLEY | ASSISTANT DIRECTOR

This will be the second time Marcus has worked with Blackshaw on a full stage production, having assistant directed *Alice In Wonderland* in earlier in 2015. Marcus is Artistic Director of Cyphers, directing their productions of *Henry V* (2014 & 2015) and *Great Expectations* (2015) as well as a radio version of his *Great Expectations* adaptation; a co-production with Blackshaw. In spring 2015, he also directed a French translation of *The Diary of a Madman* by Nikoli Gogol at the Reine Blanche in Paris.

Assistant director credits include: *Miss Wilson's Waterloo* at the Finborough Theatre (2015), *Appetite* (2013), *Othello* (2010) and *The Importance Of Being Earnest* (2010).

Twitter: @mjbazley
Website: www.cyphers.org.uk

A theatre production company working in London and the surrounding areas, Blackshaw champions new writing and adaptations, but above all, strives to produce quality theatre which inspires an audience. Alongside their main productions, Blackshaw runs regular new writing nights, from which their annual Showcase Award was born. *Staying Alive* won Blackshaw's Showcase award in 2014, which led to the show's development and production.

Blackshaw's talented members and associates form an extensive network of writers, directors, actors, designers and technicians; all of whom see the value in embracing a wide range of disciplines, sharing knowledge, and supporting fellow practitioners to create great work.

Founded in 2010, Blackshaw's productions include new works; *Audience with the Ghost Finder* (May & Oct 2013, Selkirk Upstairs & Etcetera) by M. J. Starling and *Character* by Florence Vincent (May 2014 & March 2015, Selkirk Upstairs & Tristan Bates); as well as adaptations of *Gormenghast: Titus Groan* by Mervyn Peake (April 2012, The Actors' Church, Covent Garden) and *Alice in Wonderland* by Lewis Carrol (May 2014, May 2015 & July 2015, Selkirk Upstairs, Battersea Library & The British Home).

Find out more at **www.blackshawonline.com**
@BlackshawUpdate
Subscribe to Blackshaw's podcast **The Blackshaw Arts Hour**

SLOW

Surviving the loss of your world

SLOW — Surviving the Loss of your World — is a charity that supports bereaved parents. SLOW North London came about in 2007 when two bereaved mothers, Susie Hanson and Nic Whitworth, decided to provide a space where other bereaved parents could come to meet, take time out, have a cup of tea or just be with others who felt isolated in their grief. The aim at SLOW, as its name suggests, is to allow parents to grieve at their own pace and on their own time scale, and to take strength from the company and support of others; before returning to daily life and its challenges.

SLOW holds regular daytime and evening support groups for parents. The SLOWSIBS creative workshop for bereaved children is held quarterly.

Please call SLOW on **07532 432674** or look at our website **www.slowgroup.co.uk** for further information.

SLOW is a small charity with a big impact — please support us by donating at **localgiving.com/charity/slow**

·PLEASANCE·
THEATRE ISLINGTON

Pleasance Edinburgh opened as part of the 1985 Festival Fringe with two theatres facing onto a deserted courtyard-come-car-park at an unfashionable eastern end of Edinburgh's Old Town.

Thirty seasons later the Pleasance has become one of the biggest and most highly respected venues at the Edinburgh Festival Fringe, with an international profile and a network of alumni that reads like a Who's Who of contemporary comedy, drama and entertainment.

The Pleasance Theatre Islington has been one of the most exciting fringe theatres in London since it opened its doors in 1995, providing a launch pad for some of the most memorable productions and renowned practitioners of the past decade and staying true to its mission of providing a platform for the talent of the future.

POWERED BY
·PLEASANCE·
FUTURES

The Pleasance has always provided a great many artists with a platform and launch pad for their work both at the Edinburgh Festival Fringe and at Pleasance London. The Pleasance has also supported countless individuals in associated creative, administrative and technical roles. In order to bring all of this wealth of experience and support under one umbrella, The Pleasance Theatre Trust has introduced, Pleasance Futures.

Pleasance Futures offers a variety of initiatives for an array of individuals both on and off stage. From carpenters, crew, electricians to photographers, reviewers, bloggers and film-makers the Pleasance recognises how important those first opportunities in the creative industries can be.

www.pleasance.co.uk

STAYING ALIVE

Kat Roberts

For Zoe and her family

Author's Note

The play is a work of fiction but owes a great debt to narrative research in the formation of its themes. As well as accessing stories online, I spoke to Nicola Whitworth, the co-founder of SLOW; a charity that supports bereaved parents. Nic spoke to me about the group and about her own family: her husband, Tim, her son, Hamish and her daughter, Naomi, who died on 6th April 2005. This initial conversation took place as the play was in its infancy, and was instrumental in its development. Later in the writing process I spoke to Judith Chapman about her two daughters: her elder, Emily, who died on 25th March 2000, and her younger daughter (my close friend), Nadine. My conversation with Judith helped me to expand existing ideas and themes. It also served to remind me that no two experiences of grief are the same and that this story can and should live on its own. Thank you Nic and Judith for sharing your stories with me.

I'd like to dedicate the research for *Staying Alive* to:

Naomi-Grace Whitworth
and
Emily Bornor

A note on SLOW SIBS: in the run-up to the play's production, Rachel Nott and I were lucky enough to spend an afternoon doing some acting and writing with the SLOW SIBS group. We were humbled by the resilience and creativity of these young people and their sensitivity in supporting each other through the shared experience of losing a sibling. We hope to return soon.

With thanks also to the following for their generous help with technical research: Dr Hannah Davies MBChB; Anna Anderson BA Hons. Social Work & Social Policy; Toby Herniman BEng.; David Goddard BMus; Charlie Davies CEO iGeolise.

I drew on several existing works whilst researching, namely, *Four Quartets* by T.S. Eliot, *Demeter* by Carol-Ann Duffy and *The Moth: True Stories Told Live*. I also read Lucy Prebble's *The Effect* and *That Face* by Polly Stenham around the time of writing, which may have had an effect on structure.

With thanks to the following for their work on the play's development, first production and publication: Joanna Greaves; Andrew Ashford; Rachel Nott; Matt Boothman; Rosie Harrison-Poole; Nick Quinn, Laura Newman and all at The Agency; Matt Applewhite, Sarah Liisa Wilkinson and all at Nick Hern Books; Ant Alderson, Matthew Dwyer, Amy Clamp and all at The Pleasance Theatre; Matt Roberts and all at Euphita; Ellie Pitkin, Vikki Weston and all at Blackshaw Theatre Company (as listed); The cast (as listed) and Jonny McPherson (who played the part of Jack during the play's development).

A note on Blackshaw and the cast: the passion and drive of this young, unfunded theatre company, and the support they give to developing new writers is inspiring. Without them and the actors who have dedicated so much of their time to the project, there would not be a play.

A note on Pleasance Futures: The Pleasance Theatre understands so well the struggle of emerging artists and is dedicated to providing the right support to allow new writers to flourish. Most of all The Pleasance knows that theatre is about community and I am proud to be a part of theirs.

With thanks also to my teachers and peers at Canford School, Royal Holloway University of London, The Poor School, The Open University and Tamasha's Writing Masterclass with Ella Hickson. With special thanks to Stephen Davies, a great writer and teacher. Finally: personal thanks to Matt, Sez and Rob, Mum and Dad; family Davies and my friends for your eternal support. With special thanks to Charlie for our life together.

K.R.

'You can trust a human being with grief… walk fearlessly into the house of the mourning, for grief is just love squaring up to its oldest enemy.'

Kate Braestrup

Characters

MARY EVANS
JENN WILTSHIRE
JACK WILTSHIRE
NATHAN LYNCH
WILL HEMSWORTH
ADMINISTRATOR
PORTIA GEORGE
SARAH COLT
SOCIAL WORKER

Voices of children, Katy and Tom, are to be heard over the baby monitor. These should be pre-recorded.

This text went to press before the end of rehearsals and so may differ slightly from the play as performed.

Note on the Text

Where a character stops speaking due to interruption, the end of their line will be marked –

Where one character starts speaking before another has finished, the point of interruption is marked /

Where a character's line is an ellipsis (...) this notes a gesture or expression might be made by the actor in place of dialogue. This can be ignored depending on your reading.

On page 29, Nathan quotes the following from *Four Quartets* by T.S. Eliot: Quartet 4, 'Little Gidding', I, 3rd stanza: 'And what...' to '...being dead'. And then 'the intersection...' to '...never and always.'

Scene One

Mary's house – December 2010

An open-plan kitchen/lounge, usually well kept (denoted by the decor) but currently in a state of disarray. Files and piles of paper cover the coffee table; a stack of 'Order of Service' programmes are piled on the floor… some folded but mostly not; scissors, sellotape and various gift boxes and wrapping paper adorn the kitchen table; scattered at intervals are dirty mugs, bowls and plates, as if meals have been systematically eaten and the vestiges left for some time. Strung up around the lounge area and on the sideboard are birthday cards for a young boy. JENN packs away the wrapping paper and moves the used crockery from the kitchen table to the sink. She goes to the coffee table and picks up two plates and takes them to the sink. She returns to the lounge area and picks up one of the birthday cards.

JENN. These cards?

    MARY *enters, wearing funeral attire.*

MARY. Leave them.

JENN. Really?

MARY. I want to keep them.

JENN. Yes but… up?

MARY. Yes. For now. Yes.

    MARY *goes into the kitchen area and fills the kettle.*

JENN. This stuff?

MARY. Tea? What stuff?

JENN. I'll do that.

    JENN *indicates the tea.*

MARY. It's fine. What stuff?

JENN *indicates the pile of 'Order of Service' programmes.*

Oh right... I'm not... I don't... know... look, can we just have some tea.

JENN. Of course. Anything. It's anything you want.

MARY. I want to have tea.

JENN. Okay. You sit. And I'll do it.

MARY *sits. The phone rings. They look at it. It rings out.* MARY *stands and picks up the car keys.*

Where –

MARY. There's some cake in the car.

JENN. I'll get it.

MARY *exits. The front door can be heard closing.* JENN *makes the tea. She takes out the sugar but cannot find a spoon. She looks in several drawers. She opens a drawer to find a plastic spoon suitable for a child. She takes it out and looks at it for an unusual amount of time. The phone rings. The front door can be heard opening.* JENN *puts the spoon back. She puts the sugar away. The phone rings out.* MARY *re-enters carrying two identical arrangements of funeral flowers.*

MARY. Do you want some of these?

JENN. The flowers?

MARY. There are loads.

JENN. I can take them for you.

MARY. Just a bunch. You don't have to take them all.

JENN. I can get rid of them.

MARY. It seems a waste.

JENN. When Jack's mother died we gave the flowers to the local hospice patients. I'm not... I can take them and make sure they go to a place where they will be appreciated.

MARY. Milk.

JENN. …

MARY. Damn. There's no milk.

JENN *opens the fridge and takes the milk out.*

JENN. Here.

JENN *takes the lid off.*

MARY. It's off.

JENN *smells the milk. It is off.*

JENN. I have it black anyway.

MARY. Since when?

JENN. Doing a non-dairy thing at the moment.

MARY. Sugar?

JENN *stands in front of the drawer with the spoon in it.*

JENN. No thanks. There isn't any.

MARY. Really?

JENN. No.

MARY. Well… aren't I the perfect host!

JENN. That's how I like it.

MARY. You don't have to do that.

JENN. What?

MARY. You're being nice. You don't have to be nice.

JENN *shrugs. They sip their tea.*

JENN. Well… that's disgusting.

They laugh.

Beat.

MARY. There's some cake in the car.

MARY *goes to leave. The phone rings.*

For God's sake! (*Picks up the phone.*) Hello... oh sorry,
Jack... no we were ignoring you... thought you were selling
insurance... why else would the phone ring during the day?
Yes she's right here...

MARY *hands the phone to* JENN.

JENN. Hi... no we're fine... sorry it's out of battery... just
having a cup of tea. I'm not sure in terms of timings... can
you... can you just... handle that? (*Lowers her voice.*)
There's some in the fridge.

MARY *exits to her bedroom.*

Yes but he's only to have one piece... yes but then straight to
bed. I don't know... it depends... I might stay to be honest...
at least for dinner... maybe the night... no just things are a
bit... a bit of a state... okay but try not to call the landline...
every time the phone rings she thinks it's the police...
thanks... love you too. Look I've got to go... I will. I know.
I know. Bye.

JENN *hangs up.*

Shall I get this cake then?

No answer.

Mary?

JENN *grabs the car keys and exits. The front door is heard
closing.* MARY *enters from her bedroom with incredible
purpose. She has changed into jeans and a casual jumper.
She hunts around and finds her wellies. She puts them on.
She grabs her coat and puts it on almost aggressively. As she
does so her arm knocks some of the cards off the side. She
stops dead. She picks up the cards and puts them back. One
of the cards starts to sing Stevie Wonder... 'Happy Birthday
to ya, Happy Birthday to ya, happy biiiiirrrrrth–' She shuts
the card and stares at it. The front door can be heard
opening. At the sound of the door* MARY *jumps as if
awaking from a dream.* JENN *enters.*

Where are you going?

MARY. For a walk.

JENN. Shall I go with you?

MARY. No I'm fine. (*Laughs.*) I'm fine...

JENN. We could go down to the canal. It's nice and bright out still... a few hours of light left.

MARY *sits.*

You're tired. You just sit. Would you like some of this cake? Bit of a sugar boost?

MARY *looks at the card... still gripped in her hand.*

MARY. We had a cake. Spiderman. He loved Spiderman... had the PJs.

JENN. I know.

MARY....spent hours making that cake and at the last minute found a Spiderman toy to sit on the top and he spent the whole day playing with it... didn't have time to eat any cake.

JENN. They say that don't they... don't worry about buying kids expensive toys because they'll only play with the box.

MARY. Do you remember when you bought him the Wendy house?

JENN. Yes.

MARY. He moved his bed into the box it came in. He bloody loved the thing. He said his new address was: The Early Learning Centre, This Way Up, London.

They laugh. Then suddenly MARY *convulses forward like she might be sick.*

JENN. What was that?

MARY. I want to cry.

JENN. Can you?

MARY. No.

JENN. Try.

MARY. I am.

JENN. It's okay.

MARY. It comes just like that. Just a moment. It's like he's here in the room laughing with us. He's here. I mean I think he *is* here. That's why I feel this… wave. Like he's…

JENN. It's a memory. That's what memory is.

MARY. I suppose. Do you think you can talk to the dead?

JENN. How about some cake?

MARY. I'm going mad.

JENN. It's a difficult time.

MARY. You don't have to stay.

JENN. I'd like to.

MARY. You have your own… things.

JENN. Jack can deal with all that.

MARY. No really… it's okay. I might go for a walk anyway.

JENN. Shall I come?

MARY. It just hurts. You know.

JENN. I know.

MARY. It… hurts. That's not a big enough word. It's not… they need a new word… for this…

JENN. Let's go for that walk. I'll come with you?

MARY. Yes.

JENN. Yes? Let's go together. I'll put my shoes on.

JENN *does so*. MARY *stares out the window in an almost trance*.

MARY. You'll need a coat.

JENN. No.

MARY. Rain.

JENN. No.

MARY. Yes. Look.

JENN *joins her at the window.*

JENN. Oh yes! It won't be like that tomorrow.

MARY. I hope not. We like to walk in the mornings.

JENN. Tomorrow it will stop.

MARY. Tomorrow it will stop.

Scene Two

Jack and Jenn's house

A contemporary open-plan kitchen/living area kitted out with all the latest mod-cons. It is impossibly clean and meticulously trendy. Everything seems to have its place. The table is set for a dinner party. JACK is chopping vegetables for his pumpkin and carrot soup starter. A baby monitor sits on the windowsill by the kitchen sink. Through it, JENN and baby Katy can be heard.

JENN (*off*). Where's Katy gone? Where's Katy gone? (*Beat.*) Boo!

Baby Katy can be heard squealing with delight.

Where's Katy gone? Where's Katy gone? (*Beat.*) Boo!

Baby Katy squeals again.

Oh! Is that for me? Thank you very much, you gorgeous girl. Shall we have a sing-song? Shall we have a little sing-song? Are you ready?

JENN *pulls the cord on the toy. It plays 'Twinkle Twinkle Little Star'. JENN sings along to the music. Meanwhile, JACK has finished chopping and thrown all his vegetables*

*into the blender. At intervals the sound coming from the
monitor is sharply interrupted by a blast from the blender,
churning the vegetables.*

Yay! Well done, Katy! Good girl.

The doorbell rings. JACK *walks towards the door.*

Are you hungry? I bet you're hungry... let's see what we can
do about that, shall we?

JACK *runs back to the baby monitor and turns it all the way
down then goes to the front door.*

JACK. Mary! Hello! Come in. Come in! How are you?

MARY. Uh... I'm... yeah... fine I guess.

MARY *shrugs.*

JACK. It feels like it's been ages... when really it's just... a lot
going on. It was a wonderful service. Just... beautiful. I
think Henry would have liked it very much.

MARY. Yes. Thanks.

JACK. Let me take your coat.

MARY. Thanks.

JACK. I was meaning to ask you about the third hymn...

MARY. ...

JACK. In the service. Just beautiful. Where was that one from?
I don't think I've heard it before.

MARY. Um... I really can't remember what it was to be honest.

He takes her coat and hangs it up.

JACK (*off*). Just beautiful. Really must look into replacing these
hooks. They are from a cupboard which my grandmother
used to own and then Jenn was going through some
up-cycling phase...

JACK *ushers* MARY *into the lounge.*

Yes our plan is to have this all redone eventually... but... it's just time and money, isn't it? Always the way.

A pause.

I've been meaning to ask you about your garden...

JENN (*off*). Jack!

JACK. Yes!

JENN (*off*). Can you help me a minute?

JACK. Oh!... probably a stuck zip or a necklace-fastening dilemma. Won't be a tick.

JACK *darts out of the room.* MARY *looks on the fridge at the pictures the kids have drawn. A crackling sound can be heard from the baby monitor.* MARY *goes to it and turns it up. A baby can be heard goo-ing and ga-ing.*

(*Off.*) Can you hurry up!

JENN (*off*). Come here a sec.

JACK (*off*). I'm dying in there. I've just had a conversation about hallway decor... hooks... Jenny... I talked about hooks!

JENN (*off*). Look at this.

JACK (*off*). What?

JENN (*off*). Well, come and look.

JACK (*off*). Oh yes.

JENN (*off*). I'm worried.

JACK (*off*). It's a rash. Probably just a heat rash.

JENN (*off*). Are you sure?

JACK (*off*). We'll keep an eye on it.

JENN (*off*). I don't want her to scratch.

JACK (*off*). I'll get some cream tomorrow.

Beat.

Sweetheart. It's a rash… babies get rashes, they get ill. That's pretty much all they do. It's perfectly normal. You would be amazed at how resilient they are.

JENN (*off*). Yes. Okay. Sorry. I just… I worry.

JACK (*off*). I think we are all a little hypersensitive at the moment, you know? Things like this make you think, make you… it's just a rash.

JENN (*off*). Okay.

TOM (*off*). Daddy.

JENN (*off*). Hello, mister! What are you doing up?

TOM (*off*). Can I have some water?

JENN (*off*). Back to bed please, Tom.

JACK (*off*). I'll get the water and bring it to you.

TOM (*off*). Can I say hello to Mary?

JENN (*off*). Not tonight, sweetheart. You're meant to be asleep.

TOM (*off*). I wanted to give her this.

JENN (*off*). Sweetheart… not tonight.

JACK (*off*). Come on, buddy… back to bed.

JENN (*off*). I'll be down in a minute

JACK (*off*). Jenn…

JENN (*off*). What?

JACK (*off*). I don't… I don't know how to… I don't know what to say? What am I supposed to do?

JENN (*off*). We're her friends, Jack… we are supposed to *do* friendship.

Footsteps can be heard on the stairs. JACK enters.

JACK. Yep. Just as I thought… perfume crisis… so…

JENN can be heard over the monitor.

JENN (*off*). Go back to bed, sweetheart.

JACK *dives for the monitor and turns it off.*

MARY. Could I maybe have a drink?

JACK. Yes! Yes! God sorry...

MARY. Jack?

JACK. Wine, isn't it?

MARY. Jack?

JACK. White yes?

MARY. Jack?

> JACK *stops. Defeated.*

> I was hoping that in addition to losing my only child I wouldn't also have to experience the most awkward night of my life with one of my oldest friends.

JACK. God! I know... I'm... I'm a mess... I don't know what to say and I saw you and I just knew I was going to make it worse. I feel like I know you the most – you introduced me to my wife for fuck's sake and I'm here... hooks... what is the matter with me?

MARY. I promise you, you can't make it worse.

JACK. But that's... (*Breaks down slightly then quickly recovers.*) No! I won't hear it. You're going to be fine.

> JACK *turns to her. He puts his hands on both her shoulders.*

> You. Are. Going. To be. Fine.

MARY. ...

> JACK *hugs her.* JENN *enters.*

JENN. I knew it! I always knew he had a thing for you!

> *They laugh but do not separate.* JENN *bounds over to them.*

> Let me in there!

> *All three of them hug together then let go.*

> Let's get drunk!

MARY. Okay.

JACK. Wine is it, Mary?

MARY. Sorry?

JACK. White wine?

MARY. No I'm not drinking.

JENN. Not drinking... I won't hear of it.

MARY. I'm driving.

JENN. We'll get you a taxi. Won't we, Jack?

JACK. Of course we will!

JENN. Easy.

MARY. It's okay I think I'd rather...

The doorbell rings.

JENN. He's late... I'll get it!

JACK. I'm doing drinks!

MARY. Is someone else coming?

JENN. Will Hemsworth and you know... whichever socialite pair of legs he picked up on the way here.

JENN goes to the front door.

JACK. Is that okay?

MARY. I just... I thought it was just us.

General mutterings can be heard of people arriving, off, coats being taken, welcome hugs and kisses, etc....

JACK. Oh shit! I'm so sorry... you've always had a little thing for him haven't you?

MARY. What?

JACK. Old crushes die hard, eh! Tonight could be your night.

Beat.

MARY. White wine, was it?

JACK. Yes!

MARY. Yep. Bring it on.

> WILL, PORTIA *and* JENN *enter.*

PORTIA. Oh my God! It's gorgeous. Isn't it gorgeous?

JENN. Our plan is to get it all redone eventually but you know how it is. It's just...

WILL. Sure... time and money...

JENN. ...time and money. Exactly, Will. You're exactly right.

PORTIA. I think it's divine.

JACK. Will!

> *The men shake hands vigorously.*

WILL. Old chap! God it's been... how long has it been?

JACK. Too long. Far too long. You remember Mary?

WILL (*with pity*). Of course. Of course. Of course. How are you, Mary?

MARY. I'm –

PORTIA. Is there a loo?

JENN. Yes. I'll show you.

> JENN *exits, thinking that* PORTIA *is following.*

WILL. Oh, baby! You must meet. Mary.

PORTIA. Of course. Mary. Gosh. Hi.

> PORTIA *shakes her hand.*

> I was so...

JENN (*off*). Portia! The loo is this way.

PORTIA. Oh! (*Backs out of the room.*) I was so sorry to hear about... you know.

PORTIA *does a funny wave as if shooing the awkwardness away. She exits.*

WILL. So… Mary… how *are* you?

MARY. Uh –

JACK. Get you a drink, Will?

WILL *turns away from* MARY.

WILL. Yes, great.

JACK. Wine? Gin?

WILL. Great.

JACK. Which?

WILL. Both? (*Laughs at his own joke.*) Wine. Red. Thanks. So, Mary –

MARY. I'm fine thanks. How are you doing?

WILL. Great… great. (*Looks around the room.*) Oh God! You bastard… you didn't…

WILL *wanders over to* JACK *who is taking the red wine out of a wine warmer.*

I very nearly bought this the other day.

JACK. What held you back?

WILL. It's the aesthetic.

JACK. Yes! They only have chrome.

WILL. Why would a company manufacture something so marketable and then only make one model in one colour?

JACK. Yes –

WILL. I mean this is the age of variety –

JACK. I suppose if / you can afford…

WILL. I want to be able to choose the right one for *my* kitchen… not just any old kitchen, you know?

JACK. It's all a bit of / an extravagance...

WILL. You're not going to want the same wine warmer as me; Mary isn't going to want the same as you... (*To* MARY.) am I right?

MARY. Actually I just drink mine. (*Beat.*) But don't get me wrong... in *this* space... a wine warmer... it's a no-brainer.

Beat.

WILL (*to* JACK). I listened to this podcast the other day...

PORTIA *enters.*

...on consumer identity and how important it is for people to express themselves through what they buy...

JACK *and* WILL *continue their conversation.*

PORTIA (*to* MARY). There's nothing in this house that isn't perfect. Do you know what I mean?

MARY. Yes.

PORTIA. Everything is like... so thought-out?

MARY. Yes.

PORTIA. I can't imagine my house being so tidy when I have kids. What's your house like?

MARY. Smaller.

PORTIA. My granny [or nan] died once.

MARY. Just the once?

PORTIA. Yeah and I was so... *sad*... for like... weeks.

MARY. Were you close?

PORTIA. Not really. But you... you know.

A crackling sound like white noise starts coming from the baby monitor. It gets louder and louder until it drowns out the following dialogue. MARY is frozen by the noise. All else are oblivious.

JACK. Where's Jenn?

PORTIA *joins* JACK *and* WILL.

PORTIA. Just checking on the kids. Poor little Katy has a rash.

WILL. Oh no! Is she okay?

JACK. She's fine, it's just a rash.

PORTIA. God! You can't ever switch off, can you? It's totally twenty-four seven.

WILL. She *is* okay?

JACK. Jenn? You know what it's like. She'll be down in a minute. Now let's take a seat, shall we, because we are just about there. Mary. More wine?... Mary?

JACK *walks up to* MARY *and touches her arm. The white noise stops dead.*

Mary.

MARY *looks at* JACK *like she has just woken up.*

You were miles away.

Scene Three

Mary's house

A typical young boy's bedroom. A racing-car bed with a chest of toys at the end of it. Various toys and teddies have been left as if they have just been played with, frozen in time. There is a window next to the bed which has no curtains or blind. Above the window are two sets of holes on either side. Around the holes the concrete is crumbling as if the window blind has been ripped from the wall. In the corner is a rocking chair covered in a variety of MARY'*s dresses.* NATHAN *is measuring the adjacent wall. He makes notes of his measurements on a clipboard.* MARY, *who is wearing a cocktail dress over her clothes, looks on awkwardly.*

NATHAN. Plasterboard, is it?

MARY. I don't know.

NATHAN. It's not structural.

MARY. Oh no it's... superficial. It went up... it was one big room before... I'm sure of it.

He knocks on the wall.

NATHAN. Yep.

MARY. Can I get you anything?

NATHAN. No.

MARY. Let me move all these clothes.

MARY *scoops up the pile of clothes.*

I was just... trying some things on for... I'm going out to dinner. That's why I'm dressed like this. I thought you were coming earlier.

NATHAN. No. 5 p.m.

MARY. I thought you said 2 p.m.

He strokes the wall to a new spot then knocks again.

NATHAN. Yep...

MARY. Yes?

NATHAN. ...Should be fine. Can't see any problems there.

MARY. That's good. Do you mind if I just go and change quickly... I feel like an idiot.

NATHAN. Your house.

MARY *goes into her room and removes the cocktail dress.*

Now... the window. This is going to be a problem.

MARY (*off*). I see.

NATHAN. Not much of a problem...

MARY (*off*). Right.

NATHAN....but slightly more... tricky.

MARY *re-enters*.

MARY. Right.

He looks at her. Beat.

NATHAN. And when it's more tricky it's usually more...

He rubs his fingers together suggesting 'money'.

MARY. Oh! I don't care about that.

NATHAN. Okay.

He holds his hands up defensively.

MARY. I mean...

NATHAN. No. I just like to say these things straight up.

MARY. It's fine.

NATHAN. Not saying you can't pay it of course.

MARY. No I can.

NATHAN. Good.

MARY. At least... when you say expensive... how expensive
is it?

*He looks at the window. He walks up to it and squints at it
from an angle. He does a sharp intake of breathe and then
breathes out all in one go, shaking his head in mock-dismay.*

NATHAN. It's going to... ooh... I'd say you're looking at least
five hundred more than we originally thought.

MARY. That's okay I suppose.

NATHAN. Maybe a thousand.

MARY. A thousand! You said five hundred.

NATHAN. Yes... okay maybe seven hundred more.

MARY. Mmm...

NATHAN. If I can show you…

He shoves the chest of toys into the corner. MARY *recoils.*

What we've got here is a window with a concrete panel underneath. Now, quite common in these old homes… the concrete panel may contain asbestos.

He takes the teddies off the bed and flings them onto the chair.

What we would need to do –

He goes to move the bed to show her.

MARY. Oh my God. Please don't touch it! Don't touch it. I'm sorry. I… just need this to stay here. This just has to stay… right… here.

MARY *pats the bed and strokes the bed cover.*

My son… he…

NATHAN. Oh yeah… no that's… that's not a problem at all actually, yeah what I was going to say is that… the way we would take the window out would be to put a scaffold up and work from the outside of the building in order for this to… work… and we can brick it up from the scaffold side as well. That's really what we would do for health and safety anyway so that's really not a problem.

Beat.

That's really not a problem at all. And we can just cover the bed and the other furniture… yeah we can work around that no worries.

MARY. Thank you.

NATHAN. Do you wish it were you instead?

MARY. What?

NATHAN. No. Sorry.

MARY. Say that again.

NATHAN. No. That was a stupid –

MARY. No. Go on. Do I wish…? Say it just like you did.

NATHAN. Do you wish it were you instead?

MARY. That's the first thing someone's said that hasn't been complete bullshit. Yes. I wish it was me. If someone has to be dead – I wish it was me instead. That's… that's exactly what I wish. Except most of the time I feel like he's not dead… he's alive… or… not alive but still… here somehow… like… in another room playing. And I can hear him. That's why… I just… the bed… I don't want him to be cold… if he needs to… if he's tired. Apparently that's quite common. It's just… memory.

NATHAN. Have you ever seen that musical about cats?

MARY. What?

NATHAN. Do you mind if I make a phone call?

MARY. God! Yes! Please do. What's your name again?

NATHAN. Nathan.

MARY. Nathan. I'm sorry.

NATHAN. No. You've reminded me of something.

MARY. Have I?

NATHAN. Yes. That poem. The one about time and dead people.

MARY. The one about…?

NATHAN. Have you seen a musical… there's these cats but they are human size and one sings about memory and then all the rubbish and stuff is bigger so the cats look like cat size? And it's a musical… it's about cats…

MARY. Yes it's called… *Cats*.

NATHAN. That's it! My ma loves that musical… took us loads when we were kids. The same fella what wrote that, wrote this poem.

NATHAN *dials his mother's number.*

Mum... how's the... ah... Who's that fella that what wrote
Cats?... No not the musical... the book... oh yeah ... T.S.
Eliot. (*To* MARY.) T.S. Eliot.

MARY. Oh.

NATHAN. Right. What's that T.S. Eliot one about the time?
The poem... no it's on the shelf in the lounge.... well, go to
the lounge and have a look.

He looks at MARY *and rolls his eyes.*

MARY. It's really okay. I can look it up.

He puts his hand up to stop her.

NATHAN. I'm going bank on Friday so I'll sort it then... cos it
closes at four and I'm working. It's not a problem just...
Right. The one by the standing lamp. No. No. Yes that's it,
the *Four Quartets*. (*To* MARY.) The *Four Quartets*.

MARY. Great. I'll google it.

NATHAN. Now look up the bit about time... I know there's
four of them ... it's the *Four Quartets*.

NATHAN *looks at* MARY *and rolls his eyes again.* MARY
*starts laughing, incredulous at the amount of effort going
into the exchange.*

Okay... okay don't worry about it.

MARY. I can look it –

NATHAN. Just send it down here, would you?... Cos there's a
lady here what needs to read it... never you mind. Pop it in
post office on Friday when Julie takes you to hospital.
Thanks, Mum. I'll do the bank on Friday. Okay then... it's
not a problem to do it it's just I need to do it Friday cos I'll
be paid... I'm just at work but I'll call you after. Okay then.
Ta-ra-a-bit.

He hangs up.

She'll send it down.

MARY. Thank you.

NATHAN. So the window?

MARY. Right. Shall we say seven hundred more... shake on it?

NATHAN. Okay.

They shake hands. They drop their hands but stay looking at each other, neither sure what to do next. Then NATHAN *quotes a few half-remembered lines from 'Little Gidding' from* Four Quartets *by T.S. Eliot. (See Note on Text.)*

It goes something like that.

MARY. Would you like to stay for dinner?

NATHAN. Here?

MARY. Yes.

NATHAN. Tonight?

MARY. Yes.

NATHAN. Weren't you going out to dinner?

MARY. I was. Yes.

NATHAN. What about your friends?

MARY. Fuck 'em!

Scene Four

Jack and Jenn's house

The house is as before. JENN *is dressed for dinner but her hair is partially clipped up as if she has been interrupted mid-preening.* JENN *is flitting around tidying an already immaculate space.* JACK *is sitting at the table, exhausted by the exchange.*

JACK. You know what you're doing?

JENN. What? What am I doing?

JACK. You're doing that thing you always do.

JENN. What?

JACK. Selective listening.

JENN. What?

JACK. You pick out the facts that you want to hear / and then manipulate them.

JENN. You let a complete stranger watch our child. / Is that or is that not a fact?

JACK. Not a complete stranger, it was June… she's our neighbour.

JENN. That doesn't mean she's… just because she lives next door it doesn't mean she's not –

JACK. She's a retired teacher, for fuck's sake! She has chickens. Did you ever see a paedophile with chickens?

JENN. How do you know she was a teacher?

JENN *takes the oranges from the fruit basket and looks at the label. After a moment she sneaks them into the bin.*

JACK. Because I talk, Jenn. I'm sociable. I don't see every human being as a threat to National Security. I like people. I think I'm a good judge of character. And you know what… what are you doing?

JENN. I'm… I'm throwing these away.

JACK. I bought those yesterday.

JENN. They're the wrong ones.

JACK. The wrong ones? The wrong... oranges?

JENN. I told you about the organic –

JACK. It's fruit!

JENN. It's the pesticides.

JACK. That's...

JENN. There are carcinogens in the pesticides.

JACK. Are you drunk?

JENN. I'm worried –

JACK. We are the lucky ones. We have everything. I mean, don't you feel lucky? I think about Mary –

JENN. I know you do.

JACK. That's not fair.

JENN. No. It's not fair. I worry –

JACK. You said it yourself: we are her friends. We are doing friendship. You and me. Together. I just... I can't give up on her right now.

JENN. I know. But why not?

JACK. Why not?! Jenn...

JENN. I know. I know. I know...

Beat.

JACK. This is all in your head. I think with everything that's happened... it's making us feel a little bit paranoid at the moment. (*Beat.*) I didn't have much choice today. It was an emergency with a patient and you weren't picking up your phone. June is nice... she was great with Tom.

JENN. I'll send her something.

JACK. What do you mean?

JENN. To say thank you.

Beat.

It's not her fault you're an idiot.

JACK. So... what are we...

JENN. I don't know.

JACK. Okay. Are we still fighting?

JENN. Looking at the time, we might need to call a truce. I still need to do my hair.

JACK. Right.

JENN starts crying. JACK goes over and hugs her.

JENN. I'm worried.

JACK. I know.

JENN. I still worry all the time... Tom... I can't believe he saw it... I should have been there... What if he's... traumatised?

JACK. Everything is going to be okay. Nothing is ever going to happen to Tom or Katy. I promise you.

The doorbell rings.

JENN. Oh shit. My hair!

JACK. You go upstairs.

JENN (*exiting*). Shit.

JACK. I'll get it.

JACK answers the door: sounds of greetings, introductions and coats being collected. JACK enters, ushering WILL and SARAH in behind him.

WILL. How long has it been?

JACK. Too long. Far too long.

WILL. You've repainted?

JACK. Well spotted.

WILL. Very clean.

JACK. Thanks. Sarah. Drink?

SARAH. Sure. Thanks.

JACK. Wine?

SARAH. Red. / Thanks.

WILL. Yeah. Really brightens up the place.

SARAH (*aside*). I thought you said we were going to a house party?

WILL (*aside*). Did I?

SARAH (*aside*). A New Year's house party… that's what you said.

WILL (*aside*). We're in a house, aren't we?

JACK *takes the red wine out of the wine warmer.*

Sarah, let me show you this contraption. It warms the wine so it's exactly the right temperature when you drink it.

SARAH. Oh… beats the radiator.

SARAH *takes a sip of her wine.*

Certainly is warm.

JACK. I'm a little into my gadgets I'm afraid.

JENN *enters – rejuvenated.*

JENN. Hello! Hello! Hello!

WILL. Hi!

They kiss on both cheeks.

Jenn… meet Sarah.

JENN. Sarah.

They kiss cheeks.

JACK. How's the Seek / Fit Campaign?

SARAH. Hello.

WILL. Great. Great.

SARAH. Thanks for having me.

JENN. Wine?

SARAH raises her glass.

WILL. Launching across Europe next month. Then syncing with the States.

SARAH. What is it that you do?

JENN pours herself a glass.

WILL. I'm in advertising. Mainly high-end sports and leisure brands.

JACK. Did you two meet on the way here or…?

SARAH. It's our first date.

JENN. Romantic Will.

JACK. Talk about a baptism of fire.

SARAH. Oh no. It was my idea. I always think you can tell a lot about a person by their friends.

JACK. Uh-oh!

They all laugh.

SARAH. So what are you advertising at the moment?

WILL. Well… it's more marketing really. Advertising just sounds better.

SARAH. Does it?

They laugh.

WILL. We are marketing a sports smart watch… launching across Europe next month.

SARAH. Okay.

JACK. Sounds impressive.

WILL. It's been a real old slog this campaign... definitely pulled a few all-nighters. The amazing thing is that by next year of course we will have to start all over again, you know?

JACK. Right.

JENN. Why is that?

JACK. For the upgrade?

WILL. Exactly. You've got it. All the features are ready. We just need to come up with that idea that says... *you need this*. I'm just... too close to it at the moment, you know?

SARAH. But if they're ready now. Why don't you just include them now?

WILL *laughs*.

WILL. She says the sweetest things. We save the new features for the upgrade so that customers come back and buy the latest version. People want the latest version of things. It's how we distinguish ourselves from the rest of the pack. I'm simply fulfilling a need. It's psychology.

SARAH. When you say 'need'... we're not sort of putting the western world's penchant for buying shit up there with... say... an Ethiopian dying of thirst's *need* to find clean water?

JENN. Oh no of course not.

SARAH. Well... let's just ask. Will?

WILL. Well...

SARAH. Well... what?

JENN. Will! Shame on you –

WILL. I'm not saying it is the same. I'm saying that it's all relative at the end of the day. We have clean water and, in fact everything we need so we don't occupy our minds with survival. But, it's in our nature to need things. We never just settle. A good marketing campaign can generate a desire that becomes a 'need'. And when you look at it like that. What really is the difference?

SARAH *starts laughing.*

SARAH. He says the sweetest things.

JENN. I'm so curious... how did you two meet?

WILL/SARAH. Online.

The doorbell rings.

JENN. Oh! That must be...

JACK. I'll get it.

JENN. Right.

> JACK *exits. Noises can be heard of greetings, coats being taken.*

> Yes. This is our friend Mary joining us. She might be a bit... she's just going through a bit of a... but these dinners are... I hope... nice.

WILL. Sure.

SARAH. What's –

> JACK *and* MARY *enter.*

JENN. Hello, darling! How *are* you?

MARY. Good. Thanks.

> JENN *hugs her warmly.*

JENN. It's so good to see you...

MARY. I've –

JENN. Canapé?

MARY. Hi there.

> JENN *goes to fetch a tray of canapés.*

WILL. Hi. (*Shaking her hand.*) Nice to meet you –

MARY. We've met...

WILL. Yes... and this is...

SARAH. Sarah.

WILL. Sarah.

SARAH. Clearly memory is not his strong point. Nice to meet you, Mary.

MARY laughs and shakes SARAH's hand. JENN returns with her canapés.

MARY (*warmly*). Hi.

JENN. Canapé, Will?

WILL takes a canapé and pops it in his mouth. The lights change. We are now in December 2010 in a Council Register Office.

ADMINISTRATOR. I'm sorry I'm just trying to scoff down some lunch. Don't really have an official lunch break. So... I'm very sorry for your loss, Mrs Patel.

MARY. No.

ADMINISTRATOR. No? Oh dear.

MARY. Evans. Mary Evans.

He taps at his computer for an annoying amount of time.

ADMINISTRATOR. No. Oh yes. Mary Evans. Here it is. And do you have the medical certificate?

MARY takes the certificate out of her bag and hands it to him.

Okay. That's great! So, Mrs... (*Looks at his screen.*) Ms Evans... I'm going to take you through a series of standard questions. Then we will send you on your way with a Certificate for Burial and Cremation, and a Death Certificate. You can order copies of the Death Certificate from us at an extra charge of four pounds at the time of registration... that's today. After registration, for up to one month, the price of a copy certificate will be seven pounds. After this time a copy certificate will be ten pounds.

Beat.

So...

MARY. Sorry. Copy... why do I need a copy?

ADMINISTRATOR. This may be requested by other agencies when you're dealing with something like a will or pension.

MARY. He was only a child.

ADMINISTRATOR. That's fine then. Right. Okay.

He presses a few clicks of the mouse.

The person's full name as it was when they died?

MARY. Henry, Mathew, Evans.

ADMINISTRATOR. Occupation?

MARY. He was four years old.

ADMINISTRATOR. The full name, date of birth and occupation of their surviving wife, husband or civil partner... Okay nope. We don't need that one. Okay. Yes... Date of birth?

MARY. 17th November 2006.

ADMINISTRATOR. Place of birth?

MARY. Sydney.

ADMINISTRATOR. Australia. Lovely. (*Enters info into the computer.*) Yes... travelled around there myself a bit back in the day. Great beaches. Shame about the people. So... Dad is...

MARY. Not involved.

ADMINISTRATOR. Just for the record. None of my business of course.

MARY. You think?

Lights change. Present day.

JENN. Mary, what do you think? You've not commented on the house.

MARY. It's... nice.

JENN....the redecoration.

MARY. Oh. Sure. You've... re... done... the...

JENN. We've repainted.

JENN *looks at* WILL *and* SARAH.

MARY. Oh. Sorry.

SARAH. What colour was it before?

JENN. Metropolitan Light White.

SARAH. It looks kind of white at the moment.

JENN. Yes. Now it's Cricket White!

JENN *wanders off to the fridge.*

SARAH (*to* MARY). Well... how you missed that, Mary, I'll never know.

JENN. Try one of these, Mary?

MARY *takes one.*

A new recipe... gluten-free, wheat-free, dairy-free –

MARY. Taste-free.

JACK *laughs by accident.*

SARAH. Oh. It's rather good.

JACK *hands* MARY *a glass of wine.* MARY *takes it without looking.*

WILL. Delicious. I love the health-food craze. Doesn't do me any harm.

SARAH. I bet.

JENN. Have you tried Restorative Water, Will?

WILL. No I –

JENN. You will / love it.

WILL. Really? / What is it?

JACK. All a load of nonsense.

MARY *starts laughing.*

JENN. But it works –

MARY. That's the sugar.

JENN. I swear it works.

JACK. It's sugar water. There's no health benefit whatsoever.

JENN. Oh. Oh I thought. Well… it worked for me. I always was a bit gullible, wasn't I, Mary?

JENN *laughs, embarrassed. Beat.* MARY *and* JACK *look at each other.*

SARAH. How did you all meet?

JACK. At school. Well –

JENN. These two met at school. Then –

WILL. How I met Jack…

JENN. Mary.

WILL.…that's a story –

JACK. For another time –

MARY. Jenn and I met at uni.

SARAH. I see and you introduced –

JENN. Exactly. I went home with Mary for Christmas and / her mother…

JACK. The rest is history… as they say.

SARAH. It's really nice that you're all still so close.

MARY, JACK *and* JENN *take a sip of their drink.*

JENN. Sarah. I haven't given you a tour.

SARAH. Oh great.

JENN. Come with me.

WILL. I haven't seen the extension.

JENN. Yes you have. It's been there for years.

WILL. Not fully finished.

JENN, WILL *and* SARAH *exit*.

JACK. So… how was your Christmas?

MARY. Fine. How was yours?

JACK. Fun. So… what did you do, sorry? You went to your parents?

MARY. No.

JACK. They came to you?

MARY. No… I…

JACK. Mary. You didn't spend Christmas alone?

MARY. I was fine.

JACK. You could have come here.

MARY (*stern*). I didn't want to come here. (*Recovering*.) Because… I went away… with… a millionaire who I met at… the supermarket. He was very unassuming… liked to do his own shopping… kept him grounded he said.

JACK. Mary…

MARY. We sailed around the Caribbean on his yacht and played strip poker and drank champagne and had loads and loads of sex so…

Beat.

JACK. Do you want another drink?

MARY. No thanks.

JACK *opens the fridge*.

JACK. I wonder what they're up to.

MARY. Discussing the grading of bathroom tiles?

JACK. Ah! I'm just going to put this in the outside fridge for later.

JACK *removes a bottle of champagne from the fridge. The lights change. We are now in* JACK *and* MARY'*s flat; December 2000.*

MARY. Jack! What's that?

JACK. Look. It has a cork and everything. I'm so proud of you.

They kiss.

And I'm sorry about Christmas.

MARY. It's fine.

JACK. No it's not.

JACK *opens the bottle of champagne and pours two glasses.*

MARY. I'm disappearing for the best part of a year. I think you can skip a day.

JACK. That's what I mean. We should be together while we can.

MARY. It's just a day.

JACK. Christmas Day.

MARY. Well, I'm sorry, *Dr* Wiltshire... but this is the situation in which we find ourselves. You should try to be less of a hero. Overachieving is so rude.

JACK *hands a glass to* MARY.

JACK. What shall we 'cheers' to?

MARY. To you.

JACK. No. To you: Musical Prodigy.

MARY. To us... and to world domination!

JACK....and our general sense of smugness.

They cheers and drink.

MARY. Do you ever get that feeling like ... like you're a 'somebody'?

JACK. Not really.

MARY. How can you say that? You and me… we are
'somebodies'!

JACK. Cheers to that.

MARY. Christmas doesn't matter when we are so busy being
'somebodies'.

JACK. It will matter if we want to have…

MARY. What?

JACK. …

MARY. Turkey?

JACK. No.

MARY. Sex?

JACK. No. Children.

MARY. That's a bit previous, isn't it?

JACK. Is it?

MARY. I don't know.

JACK. Don't you want some?

MARY. Some? Like several?

JACK. Yes like several.

> *Beat.*

MARY. Yes. But not right now.

JACK. God. No. But some time.

MARY. Yes. Some time like… far away from this time. So let's
just put that in a box… close the box, put the box in a drawer
– close the drawer – put the drawers on eBay – see how
much we can get for them. Buy some more drawers when we
need them. Drawers are inexpensive these days.

JACK. You and eBay.

MARY. It's the future.

JACK. Oh. eBay's the future is it? I see.

MARY. Just... come to my parents' after your shift.

JACK. Done.

MARY. Or we could go...

JACK. What?

MARY. To see your dad.

JACK. No.

MARY. Just stop by...

JACK. No.

MARY. Not for long... just for a visit.

JACK. I don't want to.

MARY. A drink.

JACK. No.

MARY. A / walk?

JACK. I said no so just drop it.

Beat.

Sorry.

MARY. My fault.

JACK. None of it is your fault. Let's just bypass this for now.

MARY. I'm only worried that you're both sitting there stubbornly waiting for the other to say something. Someone has to make the first move.

JACK. Why does it have to be me?

MARY. Because you're the brave one... whether you know it or not. Sometimes it's longer to go round the mountain than straight through.

JACK. Do you hear yourself when you speak?

MARY. Yes.

JACK. You want to dig through a mountain... do you know how long that would take?

MARY. Not if you have the tools…

JACK. What tools?

MARY. Tools… for special mountain digging.

JACK. Sure.

MARY. Maybe it's not a mountain. Maybe it's more cylindrical like a caterpillar cake… very slippery edges and lots of smarties on the outside. But inside…

JACK. Straight through…

MARY. Just sponge… Yep.

JACK. Thanks, Confucius.

He kisses her.

I'll think about it.

MARY. I know. We'll move it.

JACK. Move what?

MARY. Move Christmas.

JACK. You can't move Christmas.

MARY. Why not?

JACK. It's someone's birthday.

MARY. Who? Jesus?

JACK. Yes.

MARY. He'd totally move the party if it was on a weeknight and nobody could come.

JACK. People would come. He's the Son of God.

MARY. I think you'd be surprised… people are very non-committal when they have to get up early to herd sheep. Party on a Monday night and all of a sudden it's like: 'Me and Jesus? Yeah… we really aren't that close.' And we all know how that turns out.

JACK. But you can't move Christmas.

MARY. As the hypothetical mother of several of your hypothetical children I believe anything is possible.

The doorbell rings.

JACK. Who's that?

MARY. Oh shit... I invited Jenn round for a drink.

JACK. 'Blonde' Jenn?

MARY. No.

JACK. Not '*questions*' Jenn?

MARY. Yeah... try not to call her that to her face this time.

JACK. Sometimes it's quicker to go through the mountain than be asked questions about it.

The lights change. Present day. JENN *enters followed by* WILL.

JENN. Shall we all go outside?

WILL. It's freezing.

JENN. Don't you want to see the fireworks? Put a coat on.

WILL *exits to get a coat.*

Mary, are you coming?

MARY. Yes.

JACK, MARY *and* SARAH *exit.* JENN *makes to go outside but then turns back. She clears the glasses. She takes a new cloth from under the sink and squirts some disinfectant on the table. She scrubs furiously.* WILL *enters carrying his coat.*

WILL. I think you've got that bit.

JENN. ...

WILL. Coming outside?

JENN. I'm just...

WILL. Yes. I can see.

JENN. I can't seem to stop...

WILL. Moving?

JENN. Yes.

WILL. That's hardly the table's fault. I said to Mary: 'Nice to *meet* you.'

JENN. I know.

WILL. …

JENN. Don't worry about it.

WILL. I'm an arsehole.

JENN. She's never been one to judge.

WILL. Then I forgot my date's name.

JENN. I know.

Beat.

You are a bit of an arsehole.

They laugh.

WILL. How are you sleeping?

JENN. Fine.

WILL. Jack could prescribe you with…

JENN. I'm fine. I'm fine. I'm…

WILL. Fine?

Beat. JENN *goes back to cleaning.* WILL *picks up a cloth and helps her.*

JENN. It doesn't make sense. Not a single bit of it.

WILL. Of what?

JENN. Any of it. Anything.

WILL. Get on with it anyway.

They continue to clean.

My brother nearly drowned when I was a kid.

JENN *stops cleaning.* WILL *takes a photo out of his wallet and hands it to her.*

JENN. You look very similar. What happened?

WILL. He was in the sea. I'd dared him to swim out to a buoy. It wasn't that far. I thought. He made it and he was celebrating, waving to me, and I was waving back at first... but then the waving didn't stop...

JENN. How old were you?

WILL. Ten. He was twelve. Lifeguard saved me... brought me in.

JENN. My God. Will. And your brother...

WILL. Oh yes... um... they got Matty too. They saved us both... everything was fine. But it took a while... a long time actually for everything to really be okay again.

SARAH *enters.*

SARAH. Sorry I was just on my way back from the loo.

JENN. Sarah.

SARAH. I didn't want to –

WILL. Hi.

SARAH. ...Interrupt

WILL. No you / weren't interrupting anything.

JENN. I'm going to go out and see what's going on.

JENN *exits.*

WILL. Can I get you a drink?

SARAH. Yes thanks.

WILL *pours her a drink.*

I couldn't help but overhear... I didn't realise... your brother...

WILL. I suppose it's not really a fun fact for the dating profile.

SARAH. No.

WILL. Unless you're going for the sympathy vote.

SARAH *laughs*.

Their eyes meet.

Beat.

Besides none of that was true.

SARAH. What? Your profile?

WILL. No. My brother.

SARAH. Sorry?

WILL. My brother.

SARAH. Really?

WILL. No. He hates swimming.

SARAH. That's... dishonest.

WILL. Who cares? She feels better than she did five minutes ago.

SARAH. Tell me honestly... have you ever got past the first date with anyone?

WILL. I think I have a particular personality type...

SARAH. Sociopath?

WILL. At least we agree that I'm charming.

WILL *goes to exit*.

SARAH. Wait. Your photo?

WILL. That? That came with a frame.

SARAH. Do you even have a brother?

WILL (*casually*). Not really.

WILL *exits*. SARAH *looks at the photo*. MARY *enters*.

SARAH. I hate to say this about your friend but... I think I'm on a bad date.

MARY *laughs*.

MARY. I hate to say this about your date but… he's not my friend.

They laugh.

SARAH. Oh dear.

MARY. Yep.

SARAH. It was all going so well… such a charming man when hidden behind a keyboard and now he won't stop talking about his motorbike. Is it just me or did you not picture the man of your dreams as one who talks about revving?

MARY. It wasn't number one on my desirables list.

JENN *enters and grabs the wine from the fridge*.

SARAH. When I used to think about marrying Jason Donovan, he didn't even have a house or an office… he was just my guy on a poster. Where are all the guys on the posters? Where did they go?

MARY. You could probably have Jason Donovan now if you really want him.

JENN *sidles over.*

JENN. Top up, girls?

SARAH. Yes.

MARY. Thanks.

SARAH. What do you do, Mary?

MARY. I used to be a music teacher and I played in an orchestra a little.

JENN. A little?

JACK (*off*). Jenn!

JENN. She's lying. She was a fabulous violinist.

JACK (*off*). Jenn! Come and look at this!

JENN. Excuse me I'm being summoned.

SARAH. An orchestra… That's amazing. Was it a big one?

JENN (*exiting*). The London Symphony Orchestra.

SARAH *looks amazed.* MARY *laughs, embarrassed.*

SARAH. My goodness! That's so impressive.

MARY. It was only for a few years.

SARAH. Sorry. But let me get this straight: I'm sitting in a room with someone who's played in the London Symphony Orchestra. I wish I could hear something.

MARY. I wish I could play something. I really haven't for a while.

SARAH. Did you tour?

MARY. Oh yes. A lot of travelling… New York, Sydney, we went to Singapore once.

SARAH. I've never been there before… what was that like?

MARY. Singapore? Very… clean. I'm sure there were other things but that's all I seem to remember.

SARAH. I suppose it's quite a disparate lifestyle, is it?

MARY. I had a ball to be honest.

SARAH. What a talent! I'm so jealous. And then you went into teaching? What made you give it up?

MARY. Yes. I had to give it up when I fell pregnant.

SARAH. Of course. How many kids do you have?

Beat.

MARY. Two… Ellie and… Ben.

SARAH. Awww! How old?

MARY.…Four and two.

SARAH. Wow! Sounds like a handful. Four and two. I suppose you must be looking at schools?

MARY. Yes. Well… there's a primary school behind my house actually.

SARAH. Oh that's great. You don't have to worry about catchment areas and all that nonsense.

MARY. Nope. That's why I bought the house.

SARAH. Whereabouts do you –

MARY. Excuse me.

SARAH. Are you alright?

MARY. Yes. I just need to go to the bathroom.

> MARY *goes to exit. The lights change. We are now in a hospital side room, 29th November 2010.*

SOCIAL WORKER. You can't leave, Mrs Evans.

MARY. Sorry?

SOCIAL WORKER. You can't leave right now. I'm sorry. I'm going to have to ask you to stay here where I can see you. Just for now. Until I have finished my questions. Does that make sense, Mrs Evans?

MARY. Ms… it's Ms Evans.

SOCIAL WORKER. Ms Evans. Have a seat. Please.

> MARY *does so.*

MARY. Mary. It's Mary.

SOCIAL WORKER. Mary. Can we get you something? A cup of tea? Some water?

> MARY *doesn't hear her.*

I understand that you have had a horrific experience today. I can't say how sorry I am about your son Henry. I just wanted to explain a bit about why I'm here. In the event that a child dies unexpectedly in the home… a member of the Children and Families Team is called out to talk to the parents because the local authority has a responsibility to find out about what happened. I know you must feel like you've been singled out, especially when you've already been through so much; but I promise you this is a standard procedure. My role today is to find out from you what happened to Henry, and to do that, I will need to ask you some difficult questions to rule out any possibility that Henry's death could have been prevented. I'll just say again that this is entirely a standard procedure which is stipulated in the general guidance issued to all local authorities in the country. Do you understand?

Silence.

Mary. Do you understand?

MARY. Yes.

SOCIAL WORKER. Do you feel that you are ready to proceed?

Lights change. Present day. JACK *enters followed by* WILL *and* JENN.

JACK. It's freezing out there!

WILL. Good God! Don't go out yet, ladies. It's Baltic.

SARAH. You are about ten minutes early.

JENN. I'm fine and I'm not even wearing a jacket.

SARAH. You must have your wine jacket on.

JENN. Oh yes… and it's fleece-lined. Come on, girlies… top up…

JACK. I'm closing the window.

JENN. You can't! The outdoor lights are plugged into the power socket.

JACK. Then I'm closing the blind.

JACK *exits.*

WILL. Yes. That will warm things up!

Lights change. We are in the hospital side room as before.

SOCIAL WORKER. Did you ever think of your blinds as a risk factor in the home?

MARY. Yes.

SOCIAL WORKER. Did you do anything with the blind when you thought of it as a risk?

MARY. I made sure the bed wasn't near the window and I kept the window locked except for the very top one... the small one... when the room needed some air. I fixed one of those metal things to the wall... to wrap the cord round...

SOCIAL WORKER. A cleat?

MARY. I don't know what it's called.

SOCIAL WORKER. But the blind was an old one?

MARY. It was the one in the house when I bought it.

SOCIAL WORKER. And you didn't replace the blind when you bought the house?

MARY. No. The blinds were there.

SOCIAL WORKER. Are you aware of the new blinds that have safety features in-built?

MARY. Yes.

SOCIAL WORKER. But you didn't replace it?

MARY. No. I didn't replace it.

WILL. You didn't replace it?

MARY. No. I didn't replace it.

JENN. You didn't replace it?

MARY. No. I didn't replace it.

SOCIAL WORKER. But you did attach a cleat... to wrap the blind cord up so that it would not dangle down?

MARY. Yes.

SOCIAL WORKER. And you did this with Henry's safety in mind?

MARY. Yes.

SOCIAL WORKER. Can you tell me what happened this morning just before the accident?

WILL. Did you always let your child play upstairs on his own?

MARY. Henry liked to climb on things.

Sound of blind being let down.

JACK (*off*). No. I need to know what's going on.

SOCIAL WORKER. There was another child in the house – is that right? Tom Wiltshire. Henry's friend?

JENN. I get angry sometimes. Do you ever get angry?

MARY. He thought he was Spiderman.

JACK *knocking on the door.*

JACK (*off*). Mary? Is she in there?… Tell me then if she's in there?

SOCIAL WORKER. Did you have anyone to help you when Henry was a baby?

JENN. Did you ever hurt your son?

MARY. I didn't need any help.

SOCIAL WORKER. Where were you when the accident happened?

WILL. What *really* happened?

JACK (*off*). She's my friend.

MARY. The boys must have moved the bed.

JENN. You didn't replace the blind.

MARY. Henry must have climbed onto the windowsill.

WILL. You didn't replace the blind.

MARY. He must have unravelled the cord…

The blind sound again, then white noise coming from the baby monitor. The blind sound continues on a loop and over the top a kettle starts to boil.

WILL. Did you ever forget to feed your son?

SARAH. Ten…

JENN. How did you feel after he was born?

SARAH. Nine…

JENN. Were you sad?

SARAH. Eight…

JACK (*off*). No. I need to get into that room please.

SARAH. Seven…

JENN. Did you feel sad?

SARAH. Six…

WILL. You didn't replace the blind.

SARAH. Five…

JENN. Did you put the cord around your son's neck?

MARY. No.

SARAH. Four…

    JACK *knocking at the door.*

JACK (*off*). Mary? Just tell me she's okay!

MARY. No.

SARAH. Three…

    The kettle starts to scream.

JENN. Did you let your son die?

SARAH. Two…

WILL. What really happened?

SARAH. One…

JACK (*off*). Mary!

WILL. Did you kill your son, Ms Evans? Did you kill your son?

*Tom's voice from the monitor: 'Henry's stuck.' Then... a loud
bang from the fireworks outside cut off all other noises.
JACK re-enters.*

WILL/JENN. Happy New Year!

JACK/SARAH. Happy New Year!

JENN. Why did we come inside?

WILL. Come on!

JENN. Now we have to go back outside again.

WILL and JACK exit.

SARAH (*exiting*). It's bloody freezing.

JENN. Wait. We need more champagne.

JENN grabs the bottle and stumbles outside.

(*Off.*) Come on, Mary. We are missing it!

*Fireworks can still be heard in the background. Katy starts
crying. This can be heard through the baby monitor. MARY
looks towards where JACK and JENN have just exited...
then looks up towards the crying. MARY exits to go
upstairs. Through the monitor the door can be heard
opening. MARY picks up the baby.*

MARY (*off*). Shh! Shh! Shh!

She rocks the baby back and forth.

What's all that scary noise? Shh shh shh... hush now, little
one... back to sleep.

Katy stops crying. Tom enters the bedroom.

Shh shh shh... there we go... there we go... all better now.
Tom?

TOM (*off*). I'm scared.

MARY (*off*). It's loud, isn't it? Do you want to come and sit
with me? Tom?

Tom exits the bedroom.

WILL (*entering*). I'll get it!

> WILL *goes to the table and picks up the photo. He looks at it. He puts it in his wallet. He picks up* JACK's *coat.* JACK *enters.* JACK *is about to speak when he hears* MARY *over the monitor as Tom re-enters the bedroom.*

MARY (*off*). Where did you go?

TOM (*off*). To get this.

> JACK *listens.*

MARY (*off*). What's this? Wow. Is this for me?

TOM (*off*). Yes.

MARY (*off*). What a beautiful box. What are these? Shells?

TOM (*off*). Shells. Yes.

> WILL *hands* JACK *the coat and exits.*

MARY (*off*). Wow. And let's have a look inside… A photo of you and Henry… hey! That's amazing!

TOM (*off*). You put your memories in and when you're feeling bad then you open it and you don't feel so sad.

MARY (*off*). You think Henry is in the box?

> *Tom giggles.*

TOM (*off*). No he's not in the box.

MARY (*off*). No?

TOM (*off*). He's in the trees… and the leaves.

MARY (*off*). Really?

TOM (*off*). Uh-huh…

MARY (*off*). Is that where you see him?

TOM (*off*). Uh-huh…

MARY (*off*). I'll look for him there next time.

> JACK *breaks down.*

TOM (*off*). Yeah.

MARY (*off*). Thank you for this. Can I have a hug… then we can get you back to bed?

They hug.

Thank you, Tom.

Scene Five

Mary's house

The bedroom is as before but most of the furniture is covered with plastic sheets.

NATHAN *is hard at work.* MARY *enters carrying two cups of tea. She hands one to* NATHAN.

NATHAN. Ta.

MARY. Do you mind if I sit for a minute?

NATHAN. What's with you lot always asking permission to do things in your own homes?

MARY. I suppose 'us lot' don't want to be seen to be being impolite.

NATHAN. 'Seen to be being'? Christ! Where I'm from we just say… my house, my chair. I'm sitting. And if you don't like it you can fuck off out of it!

MARY *laughs.*

MARY. Where are you from?

NATHAN. Dudley. Well, Sedgley actually. I say Dudley cos people know where it is.

MARY. Sure… and where is it?

NATHAN. Just outside Wolverhampton.

MARY. …

NATHAN. The Midlands… The north.

MARY. No I know The Midlands… well, Birmingham.

NATHAN. It's not Birmingham.

MARY. Quite a similar accent.

NATHAN. It's not Birmingham. It's the Black Country.

MARY. Okay. It's quite funny, that territorial thing, isn't it? We don't really have it so much in the south. If I was say… from Hampshire and someone said Wiltshire I think I would just say… close enough.

Beat.

No. It is quite different, your accent, actually. It got quite thick when you were speaking to your mum that first day. Does she still live there?

NATHAN. Yeah. She says I've gone posh.

MARY. Really? Sounds quite strong to me.

NATHAN. To you but not to her.

MARY. Why is she going to hospital?… I heard you on the phone…

NATHAN. Lungs.

MARY. Lungs. Is she okay?

NATHAN. Don't think so.

MARY. What about your dad?

NATHAN. Dead.

MARY. Oh God. Do you have any brothers or sisters?

NATHAN. No. Just me.

MARY. Do you want to talk about it?

NATHAN. I've had cheerier conversations.

MARY. Sorry.

NATHAN. 'Salright.

MARY. They were saying the other day... I go to this therapy... group... thing.... how trauma can send you on a certain path, especially when you're a child because everything is happening for the first time. It's like your brain writes a code based on your experience and the way that you have come to understand the world, and you follow that script without even knowing it, all the way into adulthood. The code dictates how you deal with... basically everything. That's why people find it hard to change. Their entire existence is based on assumptions they made about themselves when their brain was still forming. You can change your behaviour. It is possible. But first you have to break the code.

NATHAN. You might want to ask for your money back.

MARY. Really? It felt... hopeful. I liked the idea of being in control.

NATHAN. You are. Do what you want.

MARY. Maybe. Maybe that's a good philosophy. You seem... normal anyway.

NATHAN. So do you.

MARY. Really?

NATHAN. Yeah. For a southerner.

MARY. I feel like I'm somewhere else most of the time.

NATHAN. Where?

MARY. I don't know. It's like... everything is past and I have gone somewhere else but I still have to be here as well and I'm wandering around my old life and wearing these clothes but nothing really feels like it fits... and going to see my old friends and they're still there... just the same... but I'm not. But I look the same and I'm wearing the same clothes so they don't really seem to notice.

NATHAN. I thought seeing friends would be a comfort?

MARY. There's nothing worse than old friends. They always think they know exactly who you are.

NATHAN. Don't they?

MARY. How could they? I don't even know any more. And everything they say I'm just sitting there thinking... I don't... it's the Emperor's New Clothes! This whole... thing. It's bullshit. How can nobody else see this?

NATHAN. The whose clothes?

MARY. The Emperor's.

NATHAN. Never heard of him.

MARY. It's a story about an emperor who rides around naked and everyone talks about how amazing his clothes are because nobody wants to see that he isn't wearing any. And then this kid...

NATHAN. Sorry but... if he's the emperor why doesn't he just buy some clothes?

MARY. Good point.

NATHAN. I mean I'm not rich but I've still the wherewithal to make a trip to the high street should I require it.

MARY. There is a reason but I can't remember.

NATHAN. What's that film where there's this fella and he's just in the world and he likes computers and then he finds out the world is not the world at all but just a computer system called the matrix and the spoons bend and the people jump really high and he goes into the matrix and there's a woman with a red dress –

MARY. You're bleeding.

NATHAN. No I think it's called *The Matrix*, you know.

MARY. No. You are bleeding. Your head.

NATHAN. Shit.

MARY. Let me see.

She tries to get a look at the top of his head but cannot reach.

Sit down a second.

NATHAN. It's fine.

MARY. No. It's bleeding.

He sits.

You have stitches.

NATHAN. Yeah.

MARY. One has come undone.

NATHAN. It's fine.

MARY. No. Wait there. I have a first-aid kit.

She exits. NATHAN goes to stop her then just as quickly gives up. He sits back down then touches the top of his head where the bleeding is coming from. He winces. MARY re-enters with a little green first-aid kit.

Here we are. Easy.

She takes out a swab and dabs it onto the cut. NATHAN winces again.

Sorry.

She rubs his arm soothingly.

This is a fresh cut.

NATHAN *grunts yes.*

Did you cut yourself?

NATHAN. No.

MARY. Did someone cut you?

NATHAN *grunts.*

Is that a 'yes'?

NATHAN. Yes.

MARY. Why?

NATHAN. Dunno.

MARY. What happened?

NATHAN. Nothing.

Pause. MARY *continues to treat the wound.*

Just in a fight. Pulled a knife. Pissed... whatever I don't know. Cunt.

MARY. Did you provoke it?

NATHAN. Who cares?

MARY. You're hurt. So... me. I care.

NATHAN. It wasn't even me. He was after me. The fucking cunt!

NATHAN *stands up and starts pacing.*

MARY. Okay. Okay. Let's just...

MARY *touches* NATHAN'*s arm. He flinches.*

NATHAN. Fuck off!

MARY. I beg your pardon?

NATHAN *stops.*

My house. My room. So sit down.

NATHAN *does so, like a schoolboy.*

This is deep. But... I think the other stitches will hold. I'll put this dressing on just to stop it bleeding any more.

NATHAN *sits.*

Okay. It's okay.

She rubs his arm again. He seems to relax a little. She continues to dress the wound in silence. He calms to her touch.

All done. Good boy.

She places a hand on either side of his head and lightly kisses the dressing.

Beat.

MARY *breaks down.*

Scene Six

Jack and Jenn's house

The house is as before with three places set for dinner. Both JACK and JENN are ready. They have been ready for some time.

JACK. She said she'll come if she can. She'll see on the night.

JENN. Well, that's a great lot of use, isn't it? It is the night.

JACK. That's what she said.

JENN. So?

JACK. So don't take it out on me.

JENN. Fine.

JACK. Jenn...

JENN. No. Fine. That's fine. You know in this whole time... I don't think I have ever been invited over to hers for dinner? Not once.

JACK. Jenn...

JENN. I don't mind hosting... no that's fine. But at least show up on time... or at all.

JACK. Stop.

JENN. Do you know she still has that room. With all his clothes in it? It's barely been touched, Jack. There's something really unhealthy about that... really unhealthy.

JACK. Okay.

JENN. Don't you agree?

JACK. Yes.

JENN. We've all had hardships in our lives. I have... you have... but you've just got to get on with it.

JACK. Yes.

JENN. I mean think of Tom. Of the trauma he went through by witnessing everything that went on that day... I can't even... but here we are and we're getting on with it.

JACK. Yes.

JENN. Sitting around wallowing all the time isn't going to get you anywhere.

JACK. Yes.

JENN. I just don't do wallowing.

Beat.

Jack, are you listening?

JACK. Yes.

Beat.

JENN. What's the matter?

JACK. Why did you marry me, Jenn?

JENN. So you weren't listening.

JACK. I'm exhausted.

JENN. What do you mean?

JACK. I mean I'm... tired. Long day.

JENN. Oh.

JACK. Sorry.

JENN. I'm sorry, darling. We should have been well under way by now. You're busy, I'm busy. We've all got lives, you

know? But we always manage to show up on time. All I
wanted to do was have a nice dinner... just the three of us...

The doorbell rings.

JACK. I'll get it.

*JACK goes to the front door. The sound of greetings and
coats being taken.*

Come on through.

JACK ushers MARY into the kitchen.

JENN. Darling!

JENN greets MARY with an over-dramatic hug.

MARY. I'm so sorry I'm late...

JENN. You're not late!

MARY....Didn't want to attempt a phone call whilst I was
driving.

JENN. Of course.

MARY. House is looking great.

JENN. Yes!

MARY. New pictures in the hallway?

JENN. Yes.

MARY. Looks lovely. Is it just us?

JENN. Yes of course. I thought it would be nice just the three
of us.

JACK. Will and Sarah are on holiday.

JENN. And I thought it would be nice.

MARY. Sarah?

JENN. I know, can you believe it? They're inseparable. The
power of the internet.

JACK. Get you some wine, Mary?

MARY. Good for them.

JACK. White is it?

MARY. No thanks I'm driving.

JENN. Oh come on!

JACK. You've got to have a glass.

JENN. We'll get you a taxi. Won't we, Jack?

JACK. Yes. Easy.

MARY. No thanks. I'm driving home… I have to be up early.

JENN. What for?

MARY. I have a meeting with a local string quartet.

JENN. Oh!

JACK. That sounds exciting.

JENN. Playing the violin?

MARY. Yes. Should be good. So no drinks.

JACK. Good for you!

JENN. You don't have to audition surely?

MARY. Yes.

JENN. Why on earth would you need to audition? Don't they know who you are? Surely you can walk into some measly local string quartet.

Beat.

MARY. I think everyone auditions. It's just the way they do things.

JACK. It's great. Really great!

JENN. Yes. And who knows? Maybe then you can get back into a proper orchestra.

JACK. Shall we sit? I think we're almost there.

MARY. Great.

They sit.

JENN. I'm so glad it's warming up. Do you remember how cold
it was this time last year?

MARY. Yes.

JENN. I always feel like a different person when the sun is out.
Do you know what I mean?

MARY. Yes.

JENN. Do you know what I mean, Jack?

JACK. Yes.

JENN. Jack took Tom to the park yesterday…

MARY. How is he?

JACK. He's great… he misses you.

JENN. …and the sun was shining all day. It was perfect. Wasn't
it perfect, Jack?

Silence.

It was! And it set just as they were walking home. They
came up the path and it was like a picture – father and son.
Wasn't it?

MARY. That's nice.

JENN. Wasn't it, Jack?

Silence.

Jack?

JACK. You know what? I can't… I can't do this today.

JENN. Do what, darling?

JACK. This. Any of it.

MARY. Are you okay?

JENN. He's so tired. Let me get the drinks, Jack, you sit down.

JACK. No.

MARY. Are you not feeling well?

JENN. Jack?

JACK. No I just... I can't do this right now. Mary. Your son died.

JENN. Jack!

JACK. And I don't know what to say to you. I don't know how long it takes to be alright again... I don't know if you can be alright again. I don't know if time even exists in this. I don't know... because it never happened to me.

JENN. Jack.

JACK. I'm sorry. I'm so sorry, Mary.

JACK *stands and exits. The front door can be heard opening and closing.*

Long pause. JENN *starts clearing away the plates.*

JENN. Well... that's that then, isn't it! Another evening ruined. I hope you're happy?

MARY. Me?

JENN. He's been stressed out all week. I knew something was going to make him snap.

MARY. And that was my arrival, was it?

JENN. Your late arrival.

MARY. I sincerely apologise for turning up to a dinner I was invited to. My mistake.

JENN. Ottolenghi. That's what we were having in case you were interested. Do you know how many ingredients go into one of these Ottolenghi dishes? All ruined now. Everything ruined. Yet again. Not to worry though. I'll just sort all this out. Don't you trouble yourself...

MARY *picks up a bowl of salad and throws it on the floor.*

MARY. Fuck the fucking Ottolenghi! Every day I wake up and forget for one moment that Henry is gone. That second is the best part of my day. I sit here trying to give some semblance of normality because I can feel you willing me to move, willing me to come through this and out the other side of it. I sit here listening to you all and I'm itching... itching to grieve and you won't let me because that would be inconvenient. And so I try... not for me, for you. And every time you talk to me about the benefits of organic baby food or how Tom has a sniffle I want to slap you in the face. And every time you try to engage me in conversation about some TV show, or the price of milk or how to make the perfect chocolate soufflé I want to scream: my son is dead! I don't want some wine. My son is dead. I don't want to go shopping. My son is dead. I don't want to treat myself to a facial, or go to the cinema to watch a romcom, or grab a cocktail with you and your fucking tiresome Surrey set. Because my son is dead. My son is dead. My son is dead.

JENN. I was asking you all those things to be nice and actually, I really wish I hadn't bothered.

MARY. You don't need to be nice. Don't be nice.

JENN. Then what shall I be, Mary? You tell me as you know everything.

MARY. Be honest! Heaven forbid we have an actual conversation because that wouldn't go over too well, would it?

JENN. I don't know what you mean.

MARY. Oh you can paint your walls as many shades of white as you like. You don't fool me.

JENN. You know what... you're right. I think you do need, in some way, to start getting over it.

MARY. And that's just it, isn't it! I've passed my grieving sell-by date, haven't I? This was fine as a topic of conversation last year but now we're just going round in circles and we really need to get on with it. It's all wearing a little thin, isn't it?

JENN. Yes it is!

MARY. And what do you suggest I do, Jenn? I wake up tomorrow and forget I had a son altogether? Like with years of passing this is meant to get easier. It gets harder. Every day that goes by is just another day he's missing.

JENN. I understand it's hard –

MARY. That's just it... you don't understand... there's no way you can understand this.

JENN. It's a process.

MARY. It's not a fucking process. You want to line up the grievances and allot a certain number of years for sadness as some sort of recompense for a life and whilst you're here making a linear plan... and checking the days off a calendar until I've become dinner-party material, I've been flung into some alternate universe. There is no time here. This is who I am.

JENN. It's not who you have to be. / Not if you choose...

MARY. Oh! And how I know you think you'd have handled this differently! If it had happened to you, you'd be cheerful and strong in the face of adversity... if this had happened to you, you'd have dug down deep and found inner strength and would be soldiering on, right? If this had happened to you –

JENN. It wouldn't have happened to me!

Pause.

MARY. Finally. Thank you. Thank you for finally being honest. And if one day you are forced to realise just how wrong you are... you come and find me... because you're going to need a friend.

MARY *exits*.

Scene Seven

Mary's house

MARY *and* NATHAN *stand looking up at the new stained-glass window in Henry's room.*

MARY. I like it.

NATHAN. Yeah?

MARY. Yes.

NATHAN. When the light hits it will look…

MARY. Yes.

NATHAN.…beautiful.

MARY. Yes.

NATHAN. You won't lose the light in the room. Which is what I was worried about.

MARY. I see.

NATHAN. But it's also something to remember… well… it is what it is.

MARY. I get it. A commemoration.

NATHAN. That's what I was thinking.

MARY. I like it.

NATHAN. Not too God-dy?

MARY. No.

NATHAN. Unless you are… I never… maybe you like…

MARY. I don't… I'm not… it's not.

NATHAN. Okay good.

MARY. I like it. Thank you.

NATHAN. Good. That's good.

Pause.

Well, I guess that's…

MARY. Yes!

NATHAN. If I can just…

MARY. Yes?

NATHAN. Get the… money?

MARY. Oh yes! Sorry.

> MARY *goes to her bag and pulls out her chequebook. She hunts around for a pen.* NATHAN *waits awkwardly. She looks through every pocket of the bag a couple of times.*

Uh… let me just…

> *She spots a pen behind* NATHAN*'s ear.*

Oh! May I?

NATHAN. Sure.

> *He hands her the pen.*

MARY. I usually have one. Thanks.

> MARY *writes the cheque.*

Do I just make it out to you?

NATHAN. Yes.

MARY. I don't know your last name?

NATHAN. Lynch.

MARY. Right.

> *She rips off the cheque and hands it to him.*
>
> *Pause.*

NATHAN. I should go then.

MARY. You don't have to go straight away.

NATHAN. Got another job.

MARY. Okay. Well… I hope we can keep in touch?

NATHAN. What for?

MARY. Just to… you know… catch up?

NATHAN. Don't really do catching up.

MARY. I was hoping we could be friends.

NATHAN. Right. Well… good luck with everything.

    NATHAN *puts on his coat.*

MARY. Wait a second. Just one second. Would you wait?

    NATHAN *pauses.*

    I get that… you are just here doing a job and that happened to be in my house… but I just needed to say something and for you to understand how much you've… Where's the violin?

NATHAN. What?

MARY. There was a violin.

NATHAN. Where?

MARY. Right here.

NATHAN. Was there?

MARY. Did you move it?

NATHAN. No there wasn't.

MARY. Yes.

NATHAN. It wasn't there.

MARY. Yes it was.

NATHAN. I put everything back the way it was.

MARY. No. There was…

    She looks around the room in cupboards and under pillows.

    It was right here.

NATHAN. I'm sorry.

MARY. Where is it?

NATHAN. I don't know.

    Beat.

MARY. You took it.

NATHAN. No I didn't.

MARY. You did. You've taken it?

NATHAN. Look…

MARY. You've come into my house and taken it.

NATHAN. What?

MARY. How dare you?

NATHAN. Oh fuck off!

MARY. Give it back.

NATHAN. No.

MARY. Please give it back.

NATHAN. I haven't got it.

MARY. Why did you take it?

NATHAN. What? Oh fuck this!

NATHAN *goes to leave.* MARY *is desperate.*

MARY. Wait! It's about money, isn't it?

NATHAN. No.

MARY. If it's about money… you aren't going to get much for it.

NATHAN. Why?

MARY. It's a child's violin. Okay. I didn't know if he'd take to it so I didn't buy him an expensive one. I can give you the money you would have got I just need to have it back.

NATHAN. How much?

MARY. You won't get more than a hundred pounds for it.

NATHAN. Fuck off!

MARY. I promise you. Okay I'll give you two hundred to have it back? Three hundred? Five hundred!

NATHAN. I didn't take it, you stupid bitch.

MARY. Me. You can have me.

Beat.

NATHAN. You?

MARY. Yeah… I've seen you… looking…

She goes to kiss him.

NATHAN. What the fuck?

MARY. Give it back!

NATHAN. No!

MARY. Give it back!

NATHAN. No!

MARY. Give it back to me!

NATHAN. Why do you need it?

MARY. I don't know!

MARY *drops to the floor.*

NATHAN. Fuck this! Seriously.

NATHAN *goes to leave.*

MARY. Wait!

She rushes to NATHAN and clutches onto him.

You can take mine. Take mine instead. My violin. It's toured the world. It's worth thousands. You take mine and I'll take his back. Mine is worth… money.… lots of money… Please. Please.

NATHAN *thinks for a moment then nods. MARY exits to get her violin. NATHAN stands for a moment. He walks over to the chair and picks up one of Henry's teddy bears and looks at it. He puts it back then exits. Footsteps down the stairs can be heard and the front door closing. MARY re-enters. She surveys the empty room. She sits on the floor and opens the violin case.*

That's it, you stand up nice and tall. Strong posture. Very proud. That's it! Good boy. Now... this part goes under your chin. Like this.

She takes the violin out of the case and places it under her chin.

So your chin rests here... just here on the black bit. Now your left hand goes at the bottom down here. These bumpy bits are called the frets. And depending on where you press down, it makes a different sound. So hold one down... any one... I know it hurts a bit but your fingers get used to it. Good. Now take the bow and... here, let Mummy show you one second...

MARY *plays a single note.*

You try?

MARY *plays the note again.*

Good! You're so good already... now when... a song? Which song? Yeah let's do that one.

MARY *stops, defeated.*

Pause.

MARY *picks up the violin defiantly and plays 'Twinkle Twinkle Little Star'.*

That's it.

MARY *looks at the violin and smiles. A moment of peace.*

You've got it.

Scene Eight

Mary's house

A table and chairs in a wild but beautiful garden. The chatter and play of children can be heard from the primary school behind the house. Someone playing the violin cuts through the general noise. The violin is played perfectly... a joyful piece. Then the violin stops and a second violin attempts the same piece – erroneously. The lesson continues with the first violin playing a part of the piece and the second copying. JACK listens through an open window. The primary-school bell rings signalling the end of their break and the noise of children fades away, leaving only the sound of the two violins playing in tandem. The lesson ends. Muffled voices can be heard saying goodbye. The front door is heard closing. MARY enters the garden.

MARY. Sorry.

JACK. No.

MARY. Just had to –

JACK. It's fine.

MARY. Couldn't really...

JACK. Really...

MARY. ...cancel.

JACK. ...it's fine. I liked listening to it.

MARY. I got a little carried away. Can I get you...?

JACK. I brought some food.

MARY. Did you?

JACK. I thought we could sit.

MARY. Sure.

JACK. I brought you this.

He takes out the bowl and hands it to her. It is glued back together.

MARY. You shouldn't have.

JACK. You got us that for our wedding present.

MARY. It was the cheapest thing on the list.

JACK. We've had it for ever. It seems a shame to throw it away.

MARY. Is that supposed to be some kind of metaphor?

JACK. I don't know. Maybe.

She looks at the bowl.

MARY. I prefer it this way.

JACK. I thought you might. It can't hold anything.

MARY. It can't hold anything but at least it's honest.

JACK. Is that supposed to be a metaphor?

MARY. No it's supposed to be a 'fuck you'.

JACK. Mary…

MARY. Okay it's supposed to be a metaphor… for 'fuck you'.

JACK. This isn't how I wanted things to be.

MARY. You don't have to come here. / You asked to be here.

JACK. We're friends.

MARY. We were friends when we were kids-teenagers-whatever. The loyalty is misplaced / because of the history…

JACK. Don't say that.

MARY. It's true. I haven't needed you for a while and you haven't needed me for… ever.

JACK. I do need you.

MARY (*standing*). If something isn't there what's the point in –

JACK. No! You can't! Please, Mary. You can't leave me as well. I'm asking you – please… for the history or whatever – just… please.

MARY *sits down again.*

Pause.

MARY. What did you mean 'as well'?

JACK. What?

MARY. You said: you can't leave me... as well.

JACK. I don't... I don't know what I mean. I suppose that's the wrong word. I just meant 'don't leave'.

MARY. Oh okay. (*Beat.*) Why are you lying?

JACK. Because I said it by accident.

MARY. You said it by accident?... You wanted me to ask. So tell me.

JACK. There's nothing to tell.

MARY. Is it Jenn?

JACK. No.

MARY. Then what?

JACK. It's Henry. It isn't just you who lost something. That's the most selfish thing I've ever said. I loved that little boy... loved him. *I* miss him. *I* wish he was here. And he isn't. I can't lose him and you, it will just be unbearable. I won't survive it. That's arrogant. I know.

MARY. Grief is pretty arrogant. Grief throws perfectly good ceramic bowls on the floor.

Beat.

You do know he wasn't yours, Jack?

JACK. No but he should have been.

Beat.

MARY. No. *That's* the most selfish thing you've ever said.

JACK. I don't know how to do this. I don't know how to...

MARY. Talk?…

JACK.…everything / is coming out the wrong way.

MARY.…because you never talk. This is the first I'm hearing of any of this.

JACK. I'm sorry!

MARY. Jack!… Can I have some of that food or are you storing it for winter?

JACK. Yes of course…

JACK takes some food items out of the bag. They open them and start picking at the contents.

I was called down to A&E the other day… they needed a consult on a man with severe burns. He'd run back into a burning building. His wife and child were trapped on the second floor. He'd used the garden hose to wet his jumper and held it over his mouth. That's what they do in the movies isn't it. But what they don't tell you in the movies is… that the smoke can be almost as hot as the fire.… taking a breath of it can burn your airway. And the smoke itself is carbon monoxide. A few breaths… it knocks out your legs from under you, slurs the speech, severely affects the ability to reason, concentrate… a few more breaths and you're passed out and not long after that you're dead. So actually the firemen found him mere metres into the house… and that jumper covered in water… was burnt directly onto his face. It formed a new skin. I could barely look at him. Because when it comes down to it… we don't want to know the details of what happens to a person with severe burns. That would stop us from answering the question we need to answer to make us feel safe. Would we go back into the building to save our family? The answer has to be yes, doesn't it? We go in and we get everybody out of the house. Your house burnt down around you and we all stood outside in the fresh air saying, 'Why doesn't she just breathe?' I left you alone.

MARY. You're here now. My friend. I thought of you that day… as it was happening. The boys had been playing upstairs

together for months… they were always so good. But I kept
the baby monitor on. The last few times it had been crackling.
I knew the batteries needed to be changed but I hadn't done it.
I just… I hadn't done it. I don't know why.

JACK. That's just one of those things…

MARY. The kettle was boiling and it was getting louder. But just
before it started to scream I heard this sound. It was a very
distinct sound… I remember thinking… 'What was that?'…
then the kettle went and the phone rang. It was my mum. She
wanted to speak to Henry because she had been ill and missed
his birthday the week before. And I turned around to call him
but Tom was standing in the doorway. He looked so scared
and he said… 'Henry's stuck'… and I knew… I knew
something had gone horribly wrong. I ran upstairs… and there
he was… hanging. I pulled the whole blind off the wall and
laid him down on the floor. I thought… 'CPR… how do I do
CPR?' And that's when you came into my head. That night…
after Doug Williams' party… your first year… do you
remember? You taught me how to do CPR to the rhythm of
that Bee Gees song. Do you remember?

JACK. Yes.

MARY. And I started doing it and I was almost saying it out
loud. 'Ah! Ah! Ah! Ah! Staying alive. Staying alive. Ah! Ah!
Ah! Ah!' And then this other version of me seemed to be
looking on saying, 'What are you doing? Your son is dying
and you are singing the Bee Gees?' I ordered Tom to get my
phone and he did, Jack… he went into my bag and he found
my mobile phone and he brought it to me. He was so brave,
Jack… he was so brave. But he was gone. He was gone. He
was gone.

JACK. You think it was you.

MARY. Yes.

JACK. Don't you?

MARY. Yes.

JACK. It wasn't.

MARY. He's still gone. But then there are moments... when I'm sitting here in the sunshine and the leaves dapple the light from the trees across my face... I can sit and look at that tree for hours and feel... he's here again... not in any way I can see, not the spirit of him... just as part of me... and then I feel... grateful... he's come home.

JACK. How is he?

MARY. He's okay.

JACK. How are you?

MARY. How am I? I'm sitting in my garden with my best friend. That's how I am.

They hold hands.

Silence.

JACK. You have knobbly fingers.

MARY. All the better to hex you with.

The lights slowly fade to black with the following conversation.

I need to talk to you actually.

JACK. Oh God.

MARY. What?

JACK. Whenever you say something like that you're always about to ask me to diagnose something.

MARY. Am I?

JACK. Well, are you?

MARY. Yes as it happens. I have the strangest bump on my toe.

She takes off her shoe and holds up her foot for him to see.

Can you see it?

JACK. Yes.

MARY. What is it?

JACK. It's a toe.

MARY. Not the toe – on the toe.

JACK. It's some kind of growth.

MARY. A growth?

JACK. Might need to take the whole foot.

MARY. Hey!

JACK. It could be worse... could have happened to me.

MARY. I'm not sure I agree with your bedside manner. I hope you don't talk to your other patients like that?

JACK. You mean my *actual* patients cos you're not a patient – you're a lady on a bench with a toe.

MARY. I hope you remember you took an oath to serve and protect.

JACK. I'm not a superhero...

Blackout.

A Nick Hern Book

Staying Alive first published in Great Britain in 2015 as a paperback original by Nick Hern Books Limited, The Glasshouse, 49a Goldhawk Road, London W12 8QP, in association with Blackshaw Theatre

Staying Alive copyright © 2015 Kat Roberts

Kat Roberts has asserted her right to be identified as the author of this work

Cover image: woodleywonderworks
www.flickr.com/photos/wwworks/3020538547

Designed and typeset by Nick Hern Books, London
Printed in the UK by Mimeo Ltd, Huntingdon, Cambridgeshire PE29 6XX

A CIP catalogue record for this book is available from the British Library

ISBN 978 1 84842 521 7

Woodland CARBON
www.woodlandcarbon.co.uk
NICK HERN BOOKS
Printed on Carbon Captured paper